Air and Water

Pan-Canadian
Science Place Team

Gary Cross

Xavier Fazio

Don Kelly

Jo-Anne Lake

Denise MacDonald

Susan Martin

Kathleen Rosborough

Wayne Stewart

Barbara Wall

Scientific Accuracy

Marc Chappell B.A. Sc., M. Eng.

Scholastic Canada Ltd.

Air and Water

LESSON 1 Why Are Air and Water Important? 4

LESSON 2 How Do You Know Air Is There? 6

LESSON 3 What Makes Air Move? 8

LESSON 4 Is There Water in the Air? 10

LESSON 5 What Makes Water Move Into the Air? 12

LESSON 6 What Happens to Water in the Air? 14

LESSON 7 What Makes Rain Fall? 16

LESSON 8 How Can Air Be Different? 18

9 How Does Weather Affect Living Things? 20

10 What Materials Keep People Dry? 22

11 How Do You Use Water? 24

12 What Happens to Water Before You Use It? 26

13 What Happens to Water After You Use It? 28

14 How Do Air and Water Get Polluted? 30

Glossary 32

This symbol tells you when to write in your science journal.

This symbol shows you when to be careful.

Be Aware!

Words in **green** are explained in the glossary on page 32.

Why Are Air and Water Important?

People, animals, and plants need air and water to live. Without air, for example, most living things could not stay alive for more than a few minutes.

Think about air and water.

1 Look at these pictures. How are air and water being used?

2 Think of one other way that air and water can be used. ✏️

THINK!
What happens to plants if they don't get water?

How Do You Know Air Is There?

You cannot see air.
You cannot smell air.
Yet it is all around you.
Look at these pictures.
Where is air? What is
air doing?

Prove air is there.

1 Fill the bag with air.

2 Use the twist tie to close the bag.

3 Squeeze the bag! How does it feel? How does it look?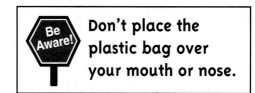

4 Open the bag. Squeeze it. What happens to the air? What happens to the bag?

You need:
• clear plastic bag (51 cm x 56 cm)
• twist tie

Be Aware! Don't place the plastic bag over your mouth or nose.

THINK
How would you describe air?

7

What Makes Air Move?

Air moves all the time. Go outside or look out the window. How do you know the air is moving?

You need:
- construction paper
- string
- ruler
- pencil
- tape
- scissors

Be Aware!

Do not touch the heater with any part of your body.

Observe air move.

1 Draw a spiral on a square piece of construction paper.

2 Cut along the dotted lines to make a round shape.

3 Cut along the solid lines to make a spiral shape.

4 Tape one end of the string to the top of the spiral. Tie the other end of the string to the ruler.

5 Hold the spiral over a heater. What happens?

The Sun, like the heater in your experiment, causes air to move.

When the Sun warms air, the air rises. Cold air then moves in to take its place.

When cold and warm air change places, the air moves. When air moves, it is called wind.

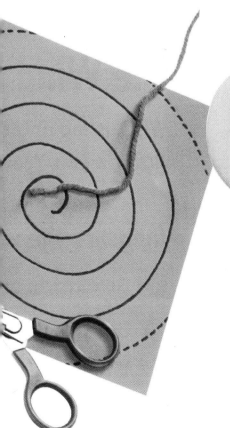

THINK!
How can you use your spiral to test for moving air?

Is There Water in the Air?

There is water all around us. It is even in the air we breathe. Water disappears into the air from lakes, rivers, and other sources of water on Earth.

Move water into the air.

You need:
• large paper plate
• 60 mL of water
• marker or pencil

1 Pour 60 mL of water onto the paper plate.

2 Trace a line around the water on the plate.

3 Look at the water each day. What do you see?

4 Trace a line around the water each day. What happens to the line?

What happened in this picture? How will the ground get dry?

THINK!
What do you call water when it changes from a liquid into a solid?

What Makes Water Move Into the Air?

Water moves into the air. This is called evaporation. What makes water move into the air? In this picture what helps water move into the air?

12

You need:
• paper towels
• water
• string
• clothespins

Test ways water moves into the air.

1 Wet two paper towels.

2 Hang one towel in the sun. Hang one in the shade.

3 Predict what you think will happen.

4 Check each towel every ten minutes. How does each towel feel? What do you think happened?

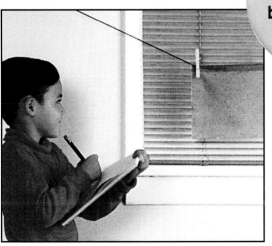

THINK!
What happens to the water on your body after you've been swimming outside?

What Happens to Water in the Air?

When water is in the air it is called water vapour. There is always water vapour in the air, but you can't see it. When water vapour rises into the sky, clouds form. Try making your own cloud!

You need:
- one large empty can
- one large empty milk carton
- ice
- warm water

Be Aware! Put masking tape along the open end of the can.

Make a cloud.

1 Fill the can with ice.

2 Fill the milk carton with warm water.

3 Hold the can with ice above the milk carton.

4 What happens? Draw what you see.

14

When warm air with lots of water vapour rises and meets cold air, the warm air cools down.

This change in the temperature of the air causes the water vapour to change back into little drops of liquid water.

Then you can see the water in the air because these little drops of water form clouds.

THINK!
What happens when you breathe out warm air on a cold day?

15

What Makes Rain Fall?

Some clouds float by without dropping one drop of rain. Others drop lots and lots of rain. What happens inside a cloud to make rain fall?

You need:
- spray bottle filled with water
- modelling clay
- cookie sheet or pie plate

Make rain.

1 Use two pieces of modelling clay to stand the cookie sheet up on a tabletop.

2 Turn the nozzle of the spray bottle to make a fine mist.

3 Spray the cookie sheet with water. What happens?

Clouds are made up of tiny water drops. These tiny water drops join together and make large water drops. When the large water drops become big and heavy they fall as rain.

Sometimes the air is so cold that water vapour changes into snowflakes instead of raindrops. Then snow falls.

THINK!
What do you call a cloud that forms on or near the ground?

How Can Air Be Different?

People are always talking about what the air is like. The air can be wet or dry, hot or cold, windy or calm. Wind, water, and heat from the sun work together to make all kinds of air conditions.

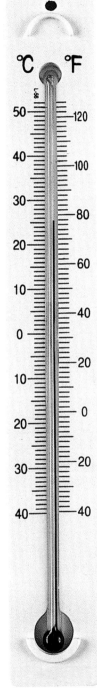

Observe air conditions.

You need:
- paper
- pencil or crayons
- thermometer

1 Observe air conditions inside and outside for a week. Write down what you see, feel, and hear.

2 How do air conditions affect you? Draw a picture to show how air conditions affect you.

THINK!
How does knowing what the weather is help you?

°F
—120
—100
80
0

19

How Does Weather Affect Living Things?

People, animals, and plants are affected by the weather. How does weather affect you?

Does it affect the way you dress? Does it affect what you can do outside?

Explore how weather affects living things.

1 Look at the pictures.

2 How does weather affect the living things in the pictures?

3 Can you think of other ways living things are affected by weather?

THINK!
How many times a year does the weather change in your part of the world?

21

What Materials Keep People Dry?

People wear special materials to keep them dry when it rains or snows. What do you wear when it rains or snows? How do these materials protect you?

You need:
- pieces of cotton, wool, paper towel, plastic wrap
- 2 measuring cups
- elastic band

Test materials for dryness.

1 Place one of the materials on top of the measuring cup. Put the elastic band around the material to hold it in place.

2 Fill a measuring cup with 15 mL of water. Pour it over the material. What happens? Does the water sit on the material? Does the water soak through the material?

3 Test the other materials. Which one will keep you the dryest?

THINK!
How are your rainboots and snowboots the same?
How are they different?

23

How Do You Use Water?

Water is part of our day-to-day lives. We use clean water to drink, cook, and wash away our body wastes. Most Canadians use about two bathtubs full of water every day. How about you? How many ways do you use water?

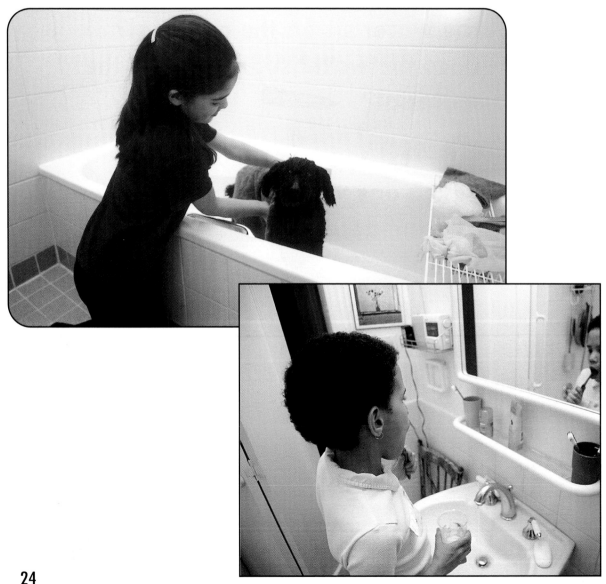

Record how you use water.

You need:
• paper
• pencil

1 With your classmates, brainstorm different ways to use water.

2 Record all the ways you use water in one week. Make a pictograph to show how many times you use water.

Number of times water used

Bathing   Washing Dog   Washing in Bathroom

THINK! How could you use less water?

What Happens to Water Before You Use It?

The water most people use is pumped from lakes or rivers into their homes. But before this water is pumped into people's homes, dirt and germs have to be removed. How is water from lakes and rivers cleaned?

Make a water cleaning system.

1 Use three plastic bottles cut in half. The top of the bottle will be part of the filter.

2 Turn the top upside down and put it inside the bottom half of the bottle.

3 Think of three different ways to clean the dirty water using the materials.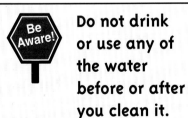

4 Plan a fair test to find out which filter cleans dirty water the best. Record the results.

You need:
- paper
- pencil
- muddy water
- 3 clear plastic pop bottles (2L)
- coffee filter
- cotton balls
- sand
- small stones or gravel
- soil
- measuring cup

Be Aware! Do not drink or use any of the water before or after you clean it.

THINK! How is the water cleaned in your community?

What Happens to Water After You Use It?

What does water look like after you use it? Where does the water go? Where does the dirt go?

What happens if water gets polluted? How are plants and animals affected?

THINK!
How could you and your family return less dirty water back to the environment?

How Do Air and Water Get Polluted?

All living things use the Earth's air and water over and over again. It is never lost or destroyed. However, it is getting harder and harder to use the Earth's air and water because of pollution.

CHEMICALS
KEEP OUT

Find causes of pollution.

1 Look at the picture.

2 How many causes of air pollution can you find.

3 How many causes of water pollution can you find.

4 What can you do to keep the Earth's air and water clean?

THINK!
How can air pollution change the weather?

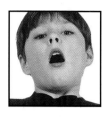

air
[ayr]

The mixture of gases that surrounds the Earth.

cloud
[klowd]

A mass of tiny water drops floating in the air.

evaporate
[ih-VAH-pore-ATE]

To change from a liquid into a gas. For example, when water moves into the air.

ice
[ice]

Solid or frozen water.

pollution
[PUHL-LOO-shun]

Pollution is waste or leftover material that can spoil clean air, water, land, or other natural resources.

rain
[rane]

Clouds form when water vapour in air changes to water droplets. Rain falls when the water droplets join together.

snow
[snoh]

Snow is frozen water droplets. When a cloud is very cold, water vapour changes to tiny ice particles which grow together to form snowflakes.